AF782539

SAP® IT Service & Application Management

SAP PRESS

SAP PRESS is issued by Bernhard Hochlehnert, SAP AG.

SAP PRESS is a joint initiative of SAP and Galileo Press. The know-how offered by SAP specialists combined with the expertise of the publishing house Galileo Press offers the reader expert books in the field. SAP PRESS features first-hand information and expert advice, and provides useful skills for professional decision-making.

SAP PRESS offers a variety of books on technical and business related topics for the SAP user. For further information, please visit our website:
www.sap-press.com.

Vital Anderhub
Service Level Management—
the ITIL process in SAP operations
SAP PRESS Essentials 21
2006, approx. 90 pp., ISBN 1-59229-103-1

Mißbach, Sosnitzka, Wilhelm, Stelzel
SAP System Operations
2003, 355 pp., ISBN 1-59229-025-8

Sabine Schöler, Liane Will

SAP® IT Service & Application Management

Galileo Press

© 2006 by Galileo Press

SAP PRESS is an imprint of Galileo Press, Fort Lee (NJ), USA
Bonn, Germany

German Edition first published 2006 by Galileo Press.

All rights reserved. Neither this publication nor any part of it may be copied or reproduced in any form or by any means or translated into another language, without the prior consent of Galileo Press, Rheinwerkallee 4, 53227 Bonn, Germany.

Galileo Press makes no warranties or representations with respect to the content hereof and specifically disclaims any implied warranties of merchantability or fitness for any particular purpose. Galileo Press assumes no responsibility for any errors that may appear in this publication.

Translation Document Service Center GmbH, Berlin, Germany
Copy Editor John Parker, UCG, Inc., Boston, MA
Layout and typesetting Steffi Ehrentraut
Cover Design Silke Braun
Printed in Germany

ISBN 1-59229-094-9
ISBN 13 978-1-59229-094-9

1st edition 2006

All of the screenshots and graphics reproduced in this book are subject to copyright © SAP AG, Dietmar-Hopp-Allee 16, 69190 Walldorf, Germany.

SAP, the SAP logo, mySAP, SAP NetWeaver, mySAP Business Suite, mySAP.com, SAP R/3, SAP R/2, SAP B2B, SAPtronic, SAPscript, SAP BW, SAP CRM, SAP EarlyWatch, SAP ArchiveLink, SAP GUI, SAP Business Workflow, SAP Business Engineer, SAP Business Navigator, SAP Business Framework, SAP Business Infor-mation Warehouse, SAP inter-enterprise solutions, SAP APO, AcceleratedSAP, InterSAP, SAPoffice, SAPfind, SAPfile, SAPtime, SAPmail, SAPaccess, SAP-EDI, R/3 Retail, Accelerated HR, Accelerated HiTech, Accelerated Consumer Products, ABAP, ABAP/4, ALE/WEB, BAPI, Business Framework, BW Explorer, EnjoySAP, mySAP.com e-business platform, mySAP Enterprise Portals, RIVA, SAPPHIRE, TeamSAP, Webflow and SAP PRESS registered or unregistered trademarks of SAP AG, Walldorf, Germany.

All other products mentioned in this book are registered or unregistered trademarks of their respective companies.

Table of Contents

Preface

This pocket guide to SAP IT Service & Application Management is based in large part on an initially internal white paper on the subject of ITIL and SAP. Dr Uwe Hommel, Senior Vice President of SAP Active Global Support, laid the foundation with his experience and ideas. Matthias Medert then drafted the first version of the white paper on this basis. This advance input helped us to go on to explore the subject in greater depth. We would therefore like to express our sincere gratitude for this. Thanks also for the contribution of Axel Hochstein and Dr Rüdiger Zarnekow of Universität St. Gallen. Of course, we would also like to extend our thanks to all other colleagues who supported us with constructive criticism and all other contributions.

1 ITIL

The release in 1989 of the first version of the Information Technology Infrastructure Library (ITIL) from the Central Computer and Telecommunications Agency (CCTA) laid the groundwork for the quality standards demanded today in IT service management. ITIL has established itself as *the* generic framework for IT organizations.

Since its inception, local ITIL organizations have taken up the task of expanding and continually updating the Best Practices set forth in ITIL. Today, ITIL comprises the fields of *Service Support*, *Service Delivery*, *Application Management*, *ICT Infrastructure Management*, *Software Asset Management*, *Business Perspective,* and *Security Management*. In addition, the volume *Planning to Implement Service Management* presented notes on implementing ITIL-compliant IT service management. This established ITIL as a universal standard for IT management. The challenge in IT management, however, lies in applying these universal Best Practices to the concrete circumstances facing individual companies.

2 SAP Life Cycle Framework and ITIL

It is no longer possible to measure the success of application-development or application-integration solely in terms of meeting deadlines or staying within budgets. Rather, the driving priority is to satisfy customers' needs through the planning, development, and operation of an efficient and effective solution landscape. The focus should not be placed only on implementation projects for new solutions, but on the whole life cycle of each solution.

The SAP Life Cycle Framework describes the life cycle of SAP-based solutions, as well as the support offered by SAP for each phase of the life cycle.

From the SAP standpoint, the life cycle is divided into three phases:

- **Plan**
  In the first phase, solutions and the corresponding solution landscape are planned. Applied to the ITIL world, the Plan phase comprises the ITIL phases Requirements and Design.
- **Build**
  The second phase consists in developing and implementing the solutions. In ITIL, this corresponds to the phases Build and Deploy.

- **Run**
  In the third life-cycle phase (Run), the solutions are run, maintained, further developed, and replaced, if appropriate. In ITIL, this phase comprises Operate and Optimize.

SAP has developed SAP IT Service & Application Management (ITSAM), which represents the SAP model for IT processes. SAP IT Service & Application Management is based on ITIL and forms the foundation for the SAP Life Cycle Framework.

The SAP Life Cycle Framework contains the SAP method and process standards as well as Best Practices.

Methods and Process Standards

Established methods are used to support the processes and activities within the individual life-cycle phases. These methods are concrete procedural methods and roadmaps (e.g. Solution Management Roadmap or ASAP) to achieve the desired results in the individual processes of the life cycle.

Best SAP Practices/Content

SAP leverages its long experience with procedure methods in the form of Best Practices that make use of previously achieved results and fill the methods with contents. This enables efficient and effective use of the methods. SAP Best Practices consist of promising configurations and procedures or benchmarks. The basis for the Life Cycle Framework is the SAP IT Service & Application Management. Figure 1 provides an overview of the SAP conceptualization of IT Service & Application Management.

Tools

SAP provides integrated instruments for the process models as well as for the methods used. In particular, the SAP Solution Manager, together with SAP NetWeaver, constitutes an ideal integration platform for control of the solution landscape over the life cycle of the individual solutions.

This pocket guide demonstrates how to employ the ITIL methodology while using SAP software, which tools are available to you, and how SAP AG supports you with services and support. The present pocket guide describes the fundamentals of SAP IT Service & Application Management. For best use of the pocket guide, you should be familiar with the Best Practices in ITIL.

2.1 Motivation

Many companies find themselves in the position of having the operating costs for their IT solutions infringe on their ability to make investments in innovative solutions. When you consider that more than 60 percent of the IT budget for most companies goes into operations, it is easy to see that there is little room left to boost competitive advantage through innovation. The logical conclusion is that operating costs must be reduced. This approach is followed by the majority of chief information officers (CIOs). Given increased cost pressure for consolidation, this would create the necessary breathing room for necessary investments (see Figure 2).

Figure 1 ▶
Overview of SAP IT Service & Application Management

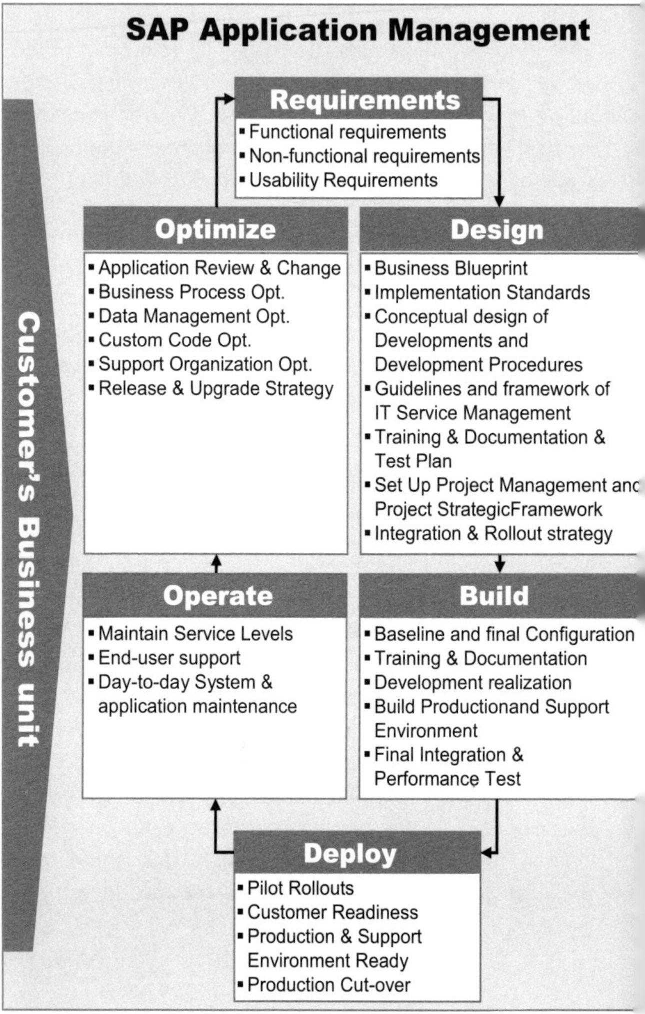
SAP Application Management
Customer's Business unit
Requirements
▪ Functional requirements
▪ Non-functional requirements
▪ Usability Requirements
Optimize
▪ Application Review & Change
▪ Business Process Opt.
▪ Data Management Opt.
▪ Custom Code Opt.
▪ Support Organization Opt.
▪ Release & Upgrade Strategy
Design
▪ Business Blueprint
▪ Implementation Standards
▪ Conceptual design of Developments and Development Procedures
▪ Guidelines and framework of IT Service Management
▪ Training & Documentation & Test Plan
▪ Set Up Project Management an
Project StrategicFramework
▪ Integration & Rollout strategy
Operate
▪ Maintain Service Levels
▪ End-user support
▪ Day-to-day System & application maintenance
Build
▪ Baseline and final Configuration
▪ Training & Documentation
▪ Development realization
▪ Build Productionand Support Environment
▪ Final Integration & Performance Test
Deploy
▪ Pilot Rollouts
▪ Customer Readiness
▪ Production & Support Environment Ready
▪ Production Cut-over

IT Service Management

Integration Processes

Design
- Technical infrastructure Planning
- Technical Architecture Design (incl. Final sizing)
- Project Installation
- Project systems support
- Operations & support strategy
- Security Requirements

Build & Deploy
- Production Installation
- Performance Test Planning
- Cut over and GoLivePlanning
- Authorizations and Security Implementation

Operations & Optimization
- Job scheduling
- Security Administration
- Application error process
- System Landscape Opt.
- Performance Review & Optimization

SAP IT Service Management

Service Support
- Incident Management
- Problem Management
- Change Management
- IT Release Management
- Configuration Management

Service Delivery
- Service-Level Management
- Availability Management
- IT Capacity Management
- Financial Management
- Continuity Management

Operations
- Job scheduling
- Print and output mgmt.
- Security Administration
- System Administration
- IT Monitoring
- Business Process Management

Customer's IT department

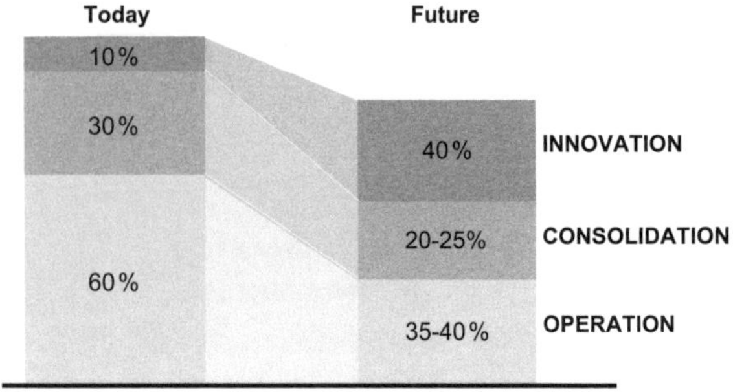

Figure 2 Current Cost Distribution and Future Requirements

Standardizing processes is a proven means of reducing costs. This increases the significance of the IT Infrastructure Library (ITIL), which has established itself as the most popular guide for processes in the field of IT service management. The resulting process transparency, process orientation, and proven Best Practices help to optimize operating costs in IT while maintaining or improving quality. The international standard ISO/IEC 20000 for IT service management is principally based on ITIL and is in full compliance with it.

Optimizing Operations and Modifications

High costs and considerable outlay are also incurred outside IT, especially in implementing and adjusting business applications. For this reason, achieving a comprehensive standardized model depends on incorporating those business-related aspects in the existing ITIL model. This is where SAP IT Service & Application Management comes into play. The most important business and Application Management processes will be described in regard to the life cycles of your solution landscape. SAP has added important aspects to ITIL in this regard.

Optimizing Business Processes

Higher operating costs can result not only from inefficient operation but also of ineffective business processes. Optimizing business processes can therefore also reduce operating costs. For an existing business process to be changed successfully, the change must be carried out with precision and care. Here, too, SAP IT Service & Application Management contributes to improved IT service management within ITIL.

Objectives

SAP IT Service & Application Management supports the standardization and implementation of processes and methods in business operations in order to achieve the following objectives:

- Optimizing the execution of changes with regard to time, integration, and the stability of the solution
- Minimizing implementation costs and implementation times while simultaneously improving quality and transparency
- Freeing up resources to resolve the conflict between permanent operating costs and costs for innovative investments

2.2 Capabilities of SAP NetWeaver for Optimizing Operations

SAP NetWeaver is an open integration platform that enables you to connect applications, processes, information, and people across organizational and technical barriers (see Figure 3). The service-oriented architecture (SOA) enables you to inexpensively integrate components or solutions. SAP NetWeaver's open functionality allows you to perform modifications without having to make fundamental changes to the technology or the software. New services can be added to the existing SAP NetWeaver architecture on any machine at any time. In contrast to a mere collection of functions, the Enterprise Service Architecture (ESA) underlying SAP NetWeaver constitutes an integral system. It offers abstraction, componentization, and selective coupling of services.

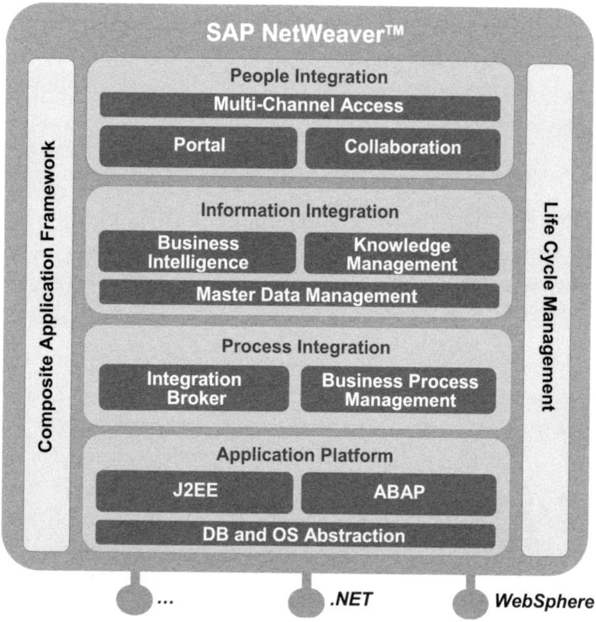

Figure 3 SAP NetWeaver as an Integration Platform

In conjunction with SAP NetWeaver, SAP IT Service & Application Management becomes the key to adjusting to constantly changing business challenges quickly, flexibly, and cost-effectively (see Figure 4). SAP NetWeaver enables you to optimally align your IT operations with your business processes. It also helps you speed up the implementation of necessary innovations while maintaining clear cost structures.

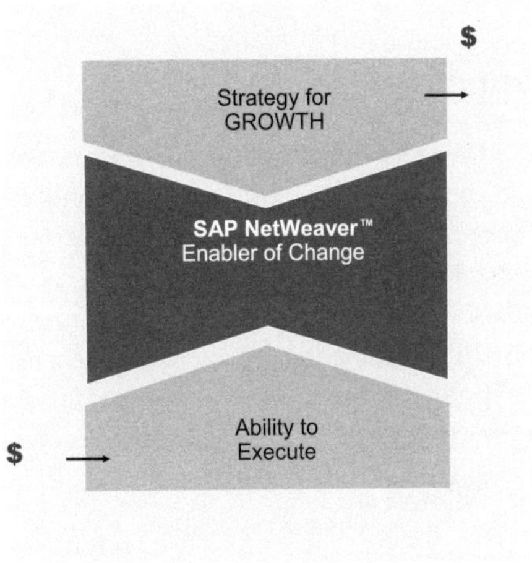

Figure 4 SAP NetWeaver as the Key to Change

2.3 Role of the SAP Solution Manager

Based on SAP NetWeaver technology, the Solution Manager is the central building block in SAP IT Service & Application Management. The SAP Solution Manager is not the only software that can be used to manage processes and phases in the application life cycle; the Solution Manager's advantage is that it brings the most important tools together in one place. This particularly simplifies the exchange of data and information across processes. The SAP Solution Manager is thus a useful tool both for the IT provider and the customer. The uses of the Solution Manager are explained in this book for each of the phases and processes. The SAP Solution Manager can also be used in conjunction with or enhanced by other tools, such as monitoring tools, for example.

2.4 Target Group

This pocket guide provides an overview of the most important aspects of application and service management and describes how SAP supports its customers through implementation and operation. This pocket guide is therefore directed at companies that want to optimize their business concepts and cost structures. This document is not conceived as a detailed examination of service management. For that purpose we recommend the widely available, classic IT Infrastructure Library and its pocket guides.

3 Structure of SAP IT Service & Application Management

While becoming familiar with SAP IT Service & Application Management (ITSAM), we recommend using the structures and names used in ITIL as an orientation. ITIL does not provide a complete solution for the efficient use of IT, but it does offer a framework of proven methods and is thus a good starting point (see Figure 5).

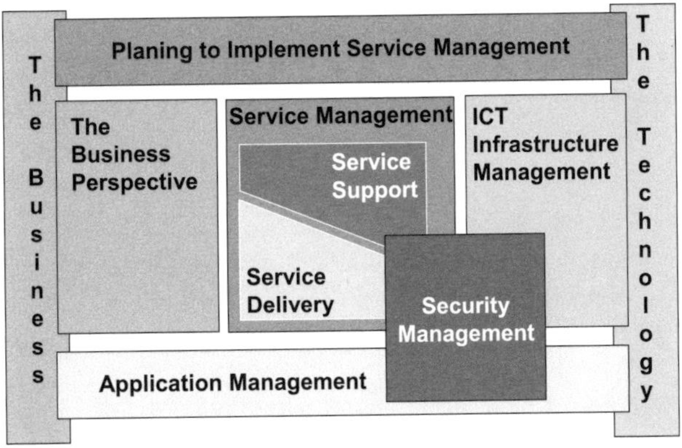

Figure 5 General Structure

We will illustrate how SAP IT Service & Application Management can improve ITIL's approach to IT application management and IT service management, as well as the interfaces between them. Three core areas emerge (see Figure 6).

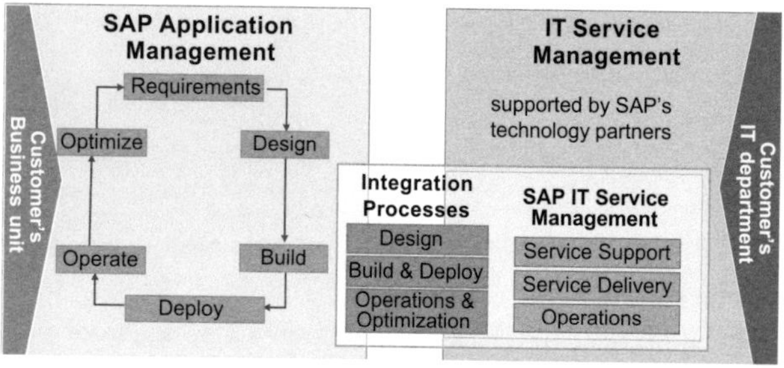

Figure 6 Core Areas of SAP IT Service & Application Management

- **SAP Application Management**
  covers all phases of an application's life cycle and is based on the ITIL model. It has, however, been greatly enhanced by SAP. It contains SAP's approach to application management and explains how SAP supports you in each phase.
- **IT Service Management**
  focuses on IT infrastructure and processes in operations. It represents the ITIL areas Service Support und Service Delivery from the point of view of the SAP operator. This reflects the pure ITIL model. A recent addition is the Operations area, which is closely tied to the other two areas. It comprises typical tasks that arise in the course of regular use of the SAP solution.
- **Integration Processes**
  deal with the most important interfaces between SAP Application Management and IT Service Management. IT

Service Management is strongly influenced by the requirements of business processes and their management. On the other hand, operational requirements must be taken into account right from the time of implementation because certain cost structures used later in operations are influenced in the implementation phase. Through Process Integration, SAP helps you manage these interfaces.

SAP NetWeaver, as the underlying software architecture, plays a significant role here. SAP NetWeaver is the framework for executing processes in SAP IT Service & Application Management.

3.1 SAP Application Management

Application Life Cycle

SAP Application Management utilizes the ITIL life cycle for application management (see Figure 7). The term "application life cycle" refers to the various phases an application goes through from the time of its inception through its official retirement. The phases Requirements, Design, and Build constitute the development stage of the life cycle. The phases Deploy, Operate, and Optimize are phases of a solution that is already being used. Optimizing changes are implemented even while the application solution is in use.

Two considerations apply to all phases of Application Management:

- For one, all activities within the application life cycle affect IT Service Management. They require corresponding modifications in the Service Support, Service Delivery, and operations areas. Changes in Application Management must take account of changes in IT Service Management, for instance in Change Management, Capacity Management, or Configuration Management. Application Management is likewise affected by changes in IT Service Management. In this case, too, relevant information must be taken into account and incorporated, if necessary, in Application Management.

- Within the individual phases of Application Management, the teams should be arranged in such a way that the core areas of IT Service Management are taken into account, in particular Operations, Support, Security, Change, Configuration, and Infrastructure. Representatives of these areas must be included in the phase-specific activities.

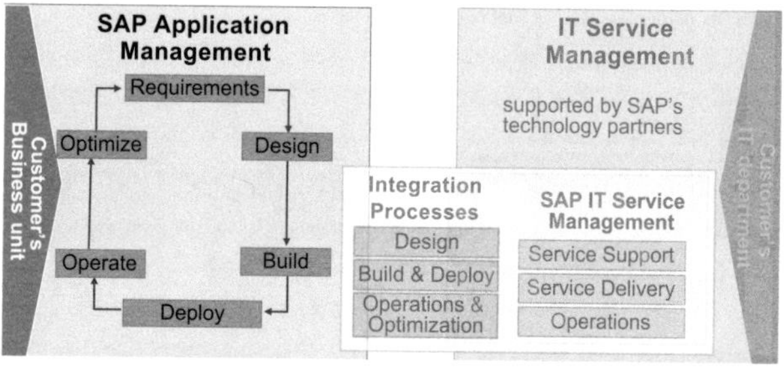

Figure 7 SAP Application Management in the Overall Structure

Service Level Management is relevant both to application management and IT Service Management. The principal objective is to define appropriate quality criteria for all phases and processes, including operations, as well as the measurement and reporting of them, so as to meet the requirements of Application Management and ensure the stable availability of the application solution.

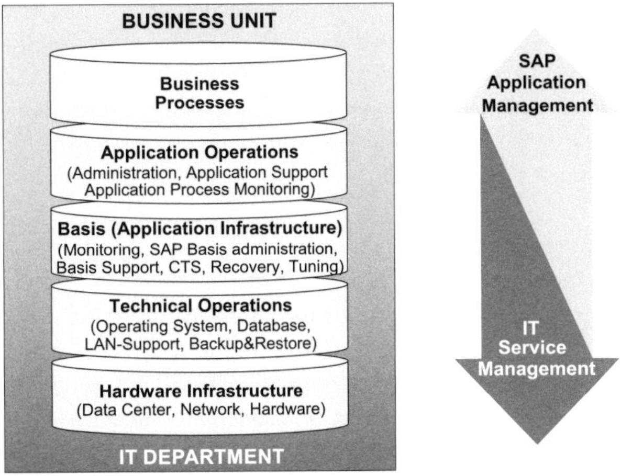

Figure 8 Technological Components and SAP Application Management

Figure 8 shows the SAP view of the various IT layers and Application Management. Occasionally, the terms used in SAP world differ from the terms used in other IT realms. Outside of SAP, people often refer to SAP software as an application. In that case, the term "application operations" would cover all primarily technical, basis-oriented activities. SAP, by contrast, distinguishes between Basis—or application—software and application operations.

In the following, we will describe the individual phases of Application Management and the support SAP provides in each phase.

3.1.1 Requirements

In the Requirements phase, development teams should work closely with key business decision-makers to determine the requirements of an application. To maximize return on investment (ROI), requirements must be weighed against the outlays required to implement them. It is sometimes more useful to optimize a business process than to map each requirement in detail from an existing process.

Requirements Category

The requirements can be grouped into three types: functional, non-functional, and end-user usability. In the Requirements phase, you should define acceptance criteria that consider all three types of requirements, as they all affect the solution design as well as the solution build activities.

Functional Requirements

Functional requirements are those that serve the implementation of a business process. What functions need to be supported by software or hardware or offered by already established solutions for a business process to be realized? These include, among other things, planned input formats and generated output formats, or how to store data so that it can be reused in subsequent steps.

Non-Functional Requirements

Non-functional requirements are often referred to as the technical requirements of an application. The technical requirements are determined by the functions planned for the business processes. The availability requirements of the business processes directly determine availability requirements on the technical systems. You have to determine the maximum acceptable time for both planned and unplanned system downtimes. Closely related to this are the performance requirements, such as response times for transactions in mission-critical processes.

To determine the technical requirements, you need precise information about the business processes, such as expected volume in terms of average and maximum expected values. Equally important is information about regularly recurring, predictable actions within the business processes, such as month-end closings or planning runs. The basic data and actions of the application directly impact the performance requirements, interface design, and sizing of the technical system landscape. Finally, it is important to set up any peripheral technology and devices in accordance with the expected business volume in the various areas of system output management. A potentially high volume of output requests, for example, must be taken into account.

Another significant, non-functional requirement for a solution is supportability. This category includes the requirement for suitable tools to analyze and resolve problems remotely. Because planned system downtimes for maintenance purposes are often limited, many support activities must be executable while the system is in operation.

Usability Requirements

But what is the use of comprehensive functionality and high availability if the system is not suited to the needs of users? It is therefore important to monitor from the outset the usability of the system in terms of the possibilities, abilities, and wishes of later users. It is important to recognize existing requirements early and include them in your considerations.

All requirements should be translated into quality criteria in service level agreements (SLAs) for the solution.

How SAP Supports this Phase
Services
▸ **SAP Custom Development** This service uses the development methods and Best Practices established by SAP to create customer-specific functions. SAP Custom Development provides direct access to SAP development teams that have the know-how and experience to plan and carry out customer-specific developments.
▸ **SAP Consulting** SAP Consulting provides support in the determination and management of requirements from both the functional and non-functional standpoints. It helps you evaluate and prioritize requirements and accompanies the process of implementing them in the software and system architecture. Rollout Management, in particular, focuses on the determination and mapping of operational requirements and accompanies their implementation.
Empowering
▸ **SAP Product Documentation** Information about how to meet functional requirements using the standard functions of SAP software is found in the SAP product documentation. You can find

this information on the SAP Service Marketplace (*service.sap.com*) on the SAP Help Portal. You also have the option of having SAP develop customer-specific functional requirements.

3.1.2 Design

Business Blueprint

In the Design phase, the requirements of an application are translated into specifications. These specifications make up what is known as the Business Blueprint. This is used to design the application itself and the environment, or operational model, that the application has to run on. It is particularly important that the design be conceived with operability and application management in mind. The design must remain flexible so that making changes does not send developers all the way back to the beginning of the design phase.

Implementation Standards

After the Requirements phase, project procedures and standards need to be defined. These standards include change-request management, support strategies, release management, and system security. Even with fixed standards, project milestones must be adhered to. This requires coordinated action by all participants in the project. To ensure coordinated action, we highly recommended you define SLAs for all areas of the project, such as project support and the project system landscape. To maintain service levels, you must already have implemented project support tools, even at this early stage of the project.

Defining the Development Project

Although there is much standard software available, you may need to enhance it or even develop your own software. For this reason, it is important to create an overriding definition of procedures and standards for the potential development project. This serves as a framework to meet business requirements that cannot be fulfilled by standard functions.

The way in which the development project enhances the standard software may influence the design. For example, if a legacy system is incorporated into the solution, you might require specific middleware.

Defining the Test Strategy

Planning appropriate test strategies is an integral part of designing a project. This may require the introduction of suitable tools. Ideally, some tests should be automatic. Tests should be planned to cover various aspects, such as the functioning of the system, integration, performance, and acceptance issues.

Planning the Documentation

Documentation is a central part of a new application. Ideally, it will be a much-used reference work throughout the life cycle of the application. Good documentation is readily available, up-to-date, and easy to understand. That requires early planning of the technical framework and rules for the documentation.

Planning for Training

If new functions are being planned in a new project, you need to consider what training courses may be necessary for future users. Only if users are made familiar with the solution in a timely way can you expect to achieve the desired acceptance and effective use.

Rules for IT Service Management

Many topics defined during the design phase can be translated into requirements for supporting and running the production solution. By this stage, you should therefore already have completed general process designs and a high-level organizational model. This is also when you want to begin to set the outline of the requirements on an SLA

Defining the Roll-Out Strategy

You also need to define the roll-out strategy for the application. There are several roll-out methodologies; you need to determine the right one for your project, for instance a phased approach or a "big-bang" deployment.

During this phase, you need to define the future solution architecture, especially the general requirements for interfaces. Part of this involves checking the compatibility of all the components within the solution landscape. You also need to identify any components that could be upgraded or replaced.

How SAP Supports this Phase

Services

- **Check of Blueprint (feasibility study)**
  The Technical Integration Test (TIC) from the SAP Safeguarding service family supports you in this phase by checking the technical feasibility and mapping your requirements in the proposed solution. It highlights potential risks and areas that can be further optimized or refined.

- **Test systems**
  SAP can provide systems temporarily for testing and demos.

Empowering

- **Defining a project for establishing a support organization, if lacking**
  SAP Empowering assessments and workshops help you define the scope of the project and support you throughout the whole process. Areas of focus include required roles and responsibilities, processes, skills profiles, and support tools. The SAP Application Management Services model offers templates and benchmark information that help you develop your support organization in the manner recommended by SAP.

Tools

- **Setting up a technical support infrastructure**
  SAP recommends you install and set up the latest version of SAP Solution Manager. This is a part of your maintenance contract with SAP. It allows you access

to programs and services that help you monitor and optimize the performance and availability of your system landscapes and minimize risks while operating your system.

- **Defining the Business Blueprint**
  SAP Solution Manager provides a function that enables you to document the business processes that you map in the SAP system. You create a project structure in which all relevant business scenarios, business processes, and process structures are structured hierarchically. You can also create project documents and assign them to individual scenarios, processes and process steps. Ultimately, you can assign transactions to each process step and thus determine the exact progression of your business processes in the SAP systems. When you have defined the Business Blueprint, you have a detailed description of your business processes and system requirements.
- **Project documentation and management**
  Project documentation is stored centrally in SAP Solution Manager. SAP Solution Manager also provides a function for integrated project management. You can use this to manage planning periods, personnel resources, and other project data.

3.1.3 Build

With the final design complete, you can now build and configure the application.

Baseline and Configuration

To implement planned developments, support and so on, technical prerequisites must be in place. These include the installation and configuration of hardware, software, development environments, and tools as planned in the Design phase.

Training and Documentation

As soon as you begin to implement the planned functions, you should also be maintaining the documentation in parallel. If you start training end users at an early stage, their feedback can help you identify and correct possible aberrations and operating or maintenance problems in the Design phase.

Development

To ensure that the application is built with later operating procedures in mind, the development team needs to consider not only the functional requirements, but also the non-functional requirements. It is therefore important to follow application-independent building guidelines and use consistent coding conventions. A standardized structure and coding style lets everyone read, understand, and manage the application easily.

Support Concept

You should use this opportunity to refine procedures and organizational responsibilities for running and supporting the production solution. Topics to be reviewed and implemented are:

- User-support strategy, including defined roles and responsibilities for end users and key users, user support infrastructure, and all support procedures and levels
- Solution management procedures, such as Business Process Management, Interface Management, and a sustainable System Management strategy
- Solution monitoring strategy for the entire solution landscape: This should contain a strategy for Service Level Management as well as a comprehensive strategy for system monitoring and business process monitoring
- Strategy for handing over systems to the organizational unit that will ultimately have to run the production solution: The handover strategy must include the scope of System Management, the requirements for the technical infrastructure handover, and a schedule for the entire handover process
- Strategy for handing over applications to the business units that will ultimately be using the solution: The handover strategy must include the scope, the requirements, and the schedule for the application handover.

After completing the operations and support strategies, you can start to put it into practice. One task is to set up user support. This includes establishing a support organization and user support infrastructure, and activating the service desk. You also need to define procedures for Business Process, Interface, and System Management as well as for program management scheduling. Monitoring is a central part of implementing the strategy. This requires Service Level Management and monitoring of business processes and systems.

Final Integration and Performance Tests

You perform comprehensive testing to make sure that the application meets all the stated requirements, that it can go live on schedule, and that risk has been minimized for running the production solution.

- Functional or user acceptance tests determine whether the system meets business needs and whether it has been developed with user requirements in mind.
- Integration tests concentrate on the interaction of different parts of the business process. The process is tested from end to end with a focus on interoperability across all affected components.
- Performance tests verify that the expected output is produced in a timely manner. They evaluate functionality under conditions of stress to simulate worst-case scenarios for the production system in terms of database size, number of users, and parallel processing of incoming/outgoing files or data.
- Regression tests might also be required for new or changed versions of the test objects. They verify that features which previously worked in the system continue to perform as they should.

How SAP Supports this Phase
Services
▶ **Managing technical risk in the implementation project** SAP Safeguarding identifies risks in your implementation project, with a special focus on integration issues.

- **Technical Consulting Services**
  Supports you while you are setting up the system and IT infrastructure and creating the administration framework (e.g. creating backup, administration and security concepts and implementing them in the system).
- **Optimizing testing**
  SAP Solution Management Optimization services optimize the way you manage and perform testing so that you can be sure your test results are reliable.
- **Analysis of the support organization**
  SAP offers analysis services to identify potential improvements to the support organization. The analyses examine whether IT Service Management is adequately prepared to deliver stable, high-performance operation over the long term. If necessary, recommendations are issued.
- **"Development laboratories"**
  Introducing central infrastructure environments and associated test and system development services in the form of "development laboratories" helps to ensure uniform quality in projects in complex system landscapes while simultaneously effectuating the consolidation of IT systems and the associated TCO reductions.
- **Hosting or outsourcing of systems**
  If you desire, SAP will operate required system infrastructure, either on-site or at SAP, for the duration of the implementation process. Responsibility for operations and the system environment is then handed over to you before the solution goes live.

Empowering
▸ **Support Tool Enabling** Support Tool Enabling encompasses the configuration of Solution Manager, including any modifications arising from the customers' wishes or developments. Support employees are simultaneously trained in the use of Solution Manager.
▸ **Setting up your support organization** SAP supports the implementation of Best Practices in support processes and structures with expert knowledge and experience. Assessments of the existing organization reveal central themes and areas in which improvements can be made.
▸ **Project documentation and -structure** You can continue to use the project documentation and project structure that you developed with the SAP Solution Manager in the Business Blueprint phase during configuration and test organization. You can display and edit the project documentation from the Business Blueprint during configuration. The project structure from the Business Blueprint is, moreover, the basis for all test plans that you create in the test organization.
▸ **User training courses** SAP offers numerous user training courses which focus on preparing end users to operate the standard software and familiarizing them with the Best Practices. These courses can be held either in the training centers or at the customer's location.

Tools

- **Configuring application systems**
  With SAP Solution Manager, you can configure application systems centrally and achieve consistent customizing with the integrated function for synchronizing customized settings. Furthermore, you can document custom code and modifications.
- **Test Workbench**
  The Test Workbench in SAP Solution Manager comprises the Test Organizer and tools for test automation. The Test Organizer supports your test administration, including the most important functions such as those for planning, reporting, and issue tracking. The transactions that you assign to process steps in the business blueprint are inserted into test plans during test-plan generation and can be processed as function tests as a means of testing the transactions. The extended Computer Aided Test Tool (eCATT) enables you to run automated tests in a complete IT solution landscape, across system and application boundaries. This is essential for efficient and accurate testing procedures.

3.1.4 Deploy

The completed and tested application is now ready to be deployed.

Production and Support Readiness

Before the switch from the implementation stage to production operation (cutover), the future production infrastructure must be in place. This encompasses not only the installation of hardware and software but also the readiness of the corresponding service processes. Production startup implies significant changes in daily operations. Any incidents that occur at this point carry much greater risks to a company's business than what occurs during implementation phases.

Checklist

It is a good idea to plan the cutover with great care, using a checklist. Each team involved in the deployment and cutover should sign off on the planned steps and provide the necessary resources for the conversion date and the days that follow the start of production. In production operation, all tasks must be carried out regularly. This is in significant contrast to the pre-production phase, in which the process steps are principally tested in regard to their functionality. The checklist should address all criteria relevant to the success of Change Management tasks, such as user training and data conversion. It should also include a time schedule and a rollback strategy in case of emergency as well as a user sign-off document.

Pilot Roll-Outs

Before the general release, it is advisable to perform pilot roll-outs. Even when the deployment process has been tested successfully in the lab, a pilot deployment in a small subset of the production system gives you the chance to optimize your cutover and even the application itself.

User Readiness

If a new application is introduced, future users must be trained in its use in advance so that they are comfortable using it in daily operations. The training courses, tests, and exercises you have planned should be completed in advance of the cutover.

Data Conversion

The start-up of a new solution is commonly associated with the transfer of old data into a new system and new structures. Since data conversion is the most critical phase during deployment, it needs to be timed and planned carefully. You should perform a cutover test that includes a test conversion and all technical cutover activities. This helps you identify issues that could prevent or hamper the go-live process. After this test, you are ready to start cutover activities for the production system, on the basis of the approved deployment plan and the checklists. These include transporting Customizing and development objects. You should verify that data conversion was successful, that the interfaces and technical infrastructure are functioning, and that the support team is able to provide the necessary system and user support.

Final Stress Test

It is often a good idea to perform one final stress test that is as realistic as possible before going live. This allows you to identify and correct any bottlenecks. However, a stress test is only truly meaningful if it mirrors the expected production operations as closely as possible. Intensive monitoring by experts is indispensable to evaluating the results of a stress test. Important project steps should be monitored with equal attentiveness. The cutover is certainly the most important and decisive event in the life cycle of a solution.

Final Approval Before Start of Production

Your production system is ready to go live when the teams responsible confirm that it is all set for live business operations, that data has been converted successfully, and that the organization and procedures of application support are ready for production operation. If user readiness is also confirmed and the cutover tasks and timetable have been verified, the steering committee can give its final approval for the start of production.

The most important milestone, production startup, is reached when business operations start to run in the new production environment. After the start of production, all project teams should carefully monitor functions and performance.

How SAP Supports this Phase
Services
▸ **Solution Management Assessment** SAP offers the Service Solution Management Assessment for the purposes of identifying and evaluating non-functional requirements and availability requirements. It analyzes the solution landscape and the most important core business processes. The result is a technical analysis of the stability and stability risk as well as of the availability and security of the core business processes. The results are then used to set future benchmarks.

- **SAP GoingLive Service**
  The SAP GoingLive Service generally consists of three separate service sessions focused on different issues. In the analysis session, about six weeks prior to going live, projected business volume is compared with the current configuration and the planned hardware resources. Based on this session, it is possible to make a reliable assessment of whether the projected business volume can be handled with the hardware and configuration. Shortly before production startup, the most important business processes are measured in terms of performance, and any final recommendations are made. Roughly four weeks after going live, actual and current values are compared in the verification session. If necessary, modifications and improvements are made to the configuration and performance.
- **Operations Enabling**
  In the case of complex multiple-system solutions or the integration of non-SAP systems, additional support is available even prior to production startup. Operations Enabling helps the customer minimize the risks of stability and performance fluctuations after the production startup of the application.
- **Support Assessment**
  SAP offers services to assess whether your support organization and system operator are prepared for the expected production startup. Ultimately, the requirements for support and system operation result from the business processes that will be operated. On this basis, an assessment is made as to whether your orga-

nization is up to the challenge in terms of know-how, established tools, and support processes.

Tools
▶ **E-learning** SAP Tutor provides interactive self-learning units, which employees can use at their workplace.
▶ **SAP Online Knowledge Products (OKPs)** These provide role-specific knowledge for SAP updates and enhancements. You can use SAP Tutor and SAP Solution Manager to create your own role-based Learning Maps.
▶ **Project documentation** SAP Solution Manager enables you to document key information regarding your project, such as descriptions of business process and functions, test scenarios, and test results.
▶ **Support tools** SAP Solution Manager is the ideal tool for your support organization and a cross-system tool for monitoring and optimizing the system landscape. SAP Application Management services present efficient ways of achieving optimal operations and support of your SAP solution.
▶ **Transition Management** Within SAP Application Management services, Transition Management deals with the transition from implementation of a solution to the permanent, stable operation of the solution in production operations. It presents suitable tools, methods and know-how.

3.1.5 Operate

Once deployed, the application is ready for regular operations. The operations and support organization is responsible for operating the business processes and the technical infrastructure. All the relevant documentation is completed and handed over to the corresponding teams. Effective operation at a high quality level significantly contributes to optimizing TCO.

Service Levels

The customer's expectations of service from the service provider—something that your internal IT department may also be considered—are usually recorded in writing within an SLA. The requisite quality criteria—so-called key performance indicators (KPIs)—and framework criteria were already defined in previous phases, so at this point it remains only to refine them and commit them to paper. All SLAs need to be measurable in order to be relevant. Measurable also means having the right tools for measuring and reporting. An SLA can cover several aspects, such as reaction times in user support, System Management, and Business Process Management.

An SLA is mutually binding. Departments can commit themselves to take part in training courses, for example, or to give notification of foreseeable deviations from the regular flow of business processes (volume, duration, scope). To ensure agreed service levels are achieved, you should monitor and document the quality criteria regularly and analyze any weak points. An SLA lives with the business processes and is thus subject to the life cycle of the application.

User Support

In order to provide satisfactory user support in terms of time and quality, you need to make sure that there is enough expertise in the support organization, that there is sufficient staffing, and that efficient procedures and tools are implemented. In addition to analyzing and resolving incidents and problems, another important task is to make diagnoses in regard to especially incident-prone components and business process steps. These diagnoses help you identify ineffective, risk-prone areas and thus areas in which improvements can be made.

Application Maintenance and Monitoring

Regular maintenance of the solution ensures fulfillment of the business process requirements. This includes regular implementation of support packages and release upgrades. Any such changes to a solution require further training of the support staff and/or modifications in the authorization concept or to interfaces. Regular, proactive performance analyses and optimization activities promote the long-term operability of the solution and enable you to react to foreseeable bottlenecks in good time.

System Management

You must schedule planned downtime for maintaining critical applications. The system administrator needs these planned downtimes to perform required maintenance tasks such as creating offline backups or changing configurations, including operating system or hardware enhancements.

Business Process Management

Analyzing and documenting core business processes is an important prerequisite to their successful operation as well as to the associated business process-oriented monitoring. This helps you achieve the expectations that have been set for the application solution. To optimize business processes, you need an appropriate integrated methodology. It is not enough to concentrate solely on individual hardware components; you must develop a comprehensive understanding of the process chain and its elements.

How SAP Supports this Phase

Services

- **Application Management**
  SAP Application Management Services support your support organization with expert help and problem solutions as well as in the continuous maintenance of the application and determination of suitable KPIs in Service Level Management.

- **Business Process Management**
  The SAP service for system administration checks the most important aspects in the operation of your solution and provides know-how and Best Practices that may be unfamiliar to you. This encompasses the main topics in SAP system administration, such as proactive and automatic monitoring, performance analysis, database management, recovery, backup, and interface setup.

- **Solution Management Optimization System Administration**
  The SAP service for system administration checks the most important aspects in the operation of your solution and provides know-how and Best Practices that may be unfamiliar to you. This encompasses the main topics in SAP system administration, such as proactive and automatic monitoring, performance analysis, database management, recovery, backup, and interface setup.
- **System monitoring**
  With SAP EarlyWatchAlert and SAP EarlyWatch Check, SAP offers the possibility of carrying out product-specific, technical measurements in SAP systems. The results are compared with the Best Practices threshold values and used to work out recommendations on how to optimize system operation. These services produce important quality criteria for the processes and results of SAP IT Service & Application Management.
- **System Management and Monitoring**
  SAP Application Management services help you manage your SAP solution and integrate interfaces. EarlyWatch Alert and EarlyWatch Check can be used to monitor performance and administration data. This enables proactive monitoring, which in turn allows you to correct performance bottlenecks and risks to data consistency in a timely fashion. You can also integrate non-SAP monitoring solutions for additional support, for instance to get a comprehensive view of the overall IT landscape or to include end-to-end perspectives (e.g. end-user-centered views).

- **Solution Operation Readiness Assessment (SORA)**
  You can use this service to identify weaknesses in the support organization and operations.

Empowering

- **Best Practices for problem resolution**
  SAP Application Management Enabling and Empowering Assessments and other workshops assess how well your support organization's Service Desk Management functions. Any problems are corrected together with you.
- **Empowering Services**
  To prepare your team for the SAP product-specific requirements, SAP offers two education and certification programs tailored to operating profiles:
  - **SAP Application Management**
    This course covers SAP Application Change Management, business process monitoring and business process performance monitoring.
  - **SAP NetWeaver Management**
    This course covers the new architecture and structure of the system landscape as well as Best Practices for system management, such as important KPIs, monitoring, problem analysis and resolution, configuration, setting up a development environment, background processing, security aspects, and user authorization profiles.

Tools

- **Monitoring and Service Level Reporting**
  Numerous monitoring functions are already integrated in the SAP software components. You can use the SAP Solution Manager to set up the central Monitoring Cockpit. From the Monitoring Cockpit you can simultaneously analyze any incidents and problems. SAP Solution Manager Diagnostics is an enhancement to the Solution Manager specially designed to serve the demands of root-cause analysis in SAP NetWeaver. With the SAP Solution Manager, you can monitor and report on service levels for systems and central business processes.
- **Service Level Reporting**
  On the basis of SAP EarlyWatchAlert evaluations and additional data from the technical monitoring apparatus provided in the Solution Manager, you can set up service-level reporting, in particular for the Applications Operations and lower-level areas (see Figure 8 earlier in this chapter).
- **Service Support**
  With the Support Desk, the SAP Solution Manager provides an end-to-end tool for executing Incident and Problem Management processes. At the same time, in Solution Manager Diagnostics the Solution Manager offers an expert tool for analyzing problems and solving them across the whole system landscape.

3.1.6 Optimize

During production operations, an IT solution is also further developed, and it becomes constantly optimized. This optimization can be triggered by the lines of business, driven by technical reasons or newly released software upgrades, and so on. Optimizing systems is crucial for keeping the operations costs down.

Change Requests

Sometimes it is necessary to make changes in production operations. Problem Management is often the catalyst. It may also become necessary to make modifications to the regular development of business processes, organization, etc. (continuous change). Likewise, the continuous optimization of procedures also requires changes (continuous improvement). In addition, a change in technical infrastructure may mean that you have to adapt the application. Changes can encompass new functions or structures, the development of new and optimized reports, and training of key users and the support organization.

Application Change Management

Once the application is in use in production operations, every change carries risks. Standardized methods and procedures, together with tests of all changes, ensure that changes are realized quickly and efficiently, minimizing the negative impact they can have on business operations. The process begins with the registration of change requests. This is followed by evaluating, managing, and monitoring the implementation. The final step involves reviewing the success of the change. Beyond the ordinary change procedure, however, errors can also require you to make quick changes to the system. An appropriate procedure is called for in these cases as well. To avoid emergencies, we recommend that you regularly implement the Support Packages released by SAP. Support Packages contain bundled corrections and optimizations for specific modules.

Optimizing Business Processes

Within your SLA, you usually define key performance indicators (KPIs) for core business processes and compile service-level reports at regular intervals. These reports identify any transactions that are not meeting your business requirements. This information should help you uncover any potential for optimization. For instance, you might be able to avoid unnecessary database access or benefit from implementing parallel processing.

Data Administration

Another area of optimization is data administration, especially database growth management and archiving. The goal of any optimization activity is to ensure that your database resources are being used efficiently by avoiding the accumulation of unnecessary data, deleting unnecessary data, and archiving business data on a regular basis. These proactive tasks help to prevent problem situations and thus reduce operating costs.

Utilization of System Resources

The server landscape required to run your SAP systems accounts for a significant portion of day-to-day infrastructure costs and administrative work. Modern approaches such as virtualization and adaptive computing make it possible to redistribute computing capacity among the respective systems during load peaks or planned or unplanned downtimes, obviating the need to maintain large standby capacities.

Optimizing User-Defined Code

As described in the design phase, it may have been necessary to extend or adapt standard functions using custom code. New releases of standard software might cover these functions. In such cases, replacing the custom code with standard code or at least encapsulating it will reduce your maintenance outlay significantly. It will also simplify certain actions, such as transporting data to production systems, distributing software, or importing Support Packages. If you cannot eliminate custom code, you might at least be able to tune it so that it meets your KPIs, such as performance, data consistency, maintainability, operability, and "upgradeability."

Optimizing the Support Organization

Optimizing the skills, procedures, and tools in your support organization allows it to respond to and resolve issues quickly and competently. Your support organization will work more proactively and be able to maintain the performance and availability of your application.

Release and Upgrade Strategy

The best practices in most industries are changing dynamically. This is accompanied by constant changes to the technology stack. As a result, application vendors offer new versions or releases of the application and you need to decide upon a release and upgrade strategy.

Upgrading can make economic sense if the new releases provide functions that your changed core business processes require. Two main aspects to consider are your rollout times and resources and the maintenance options from the application vendor.

If you decide to upgrade, you should consider all the aspects mentioned above, such as user training in the deployment phase.

How SAP Supports this Phase

Services

- **Solution Management Optimization Services**
  Figure 9 shows an overview of the available groupings and focus areas for this class of services. Primarily, these services are intended for the optimization of existing IT service processes. However, with relatively nominal changes, they can also be used to set up processes in the Operate life cycle phase.

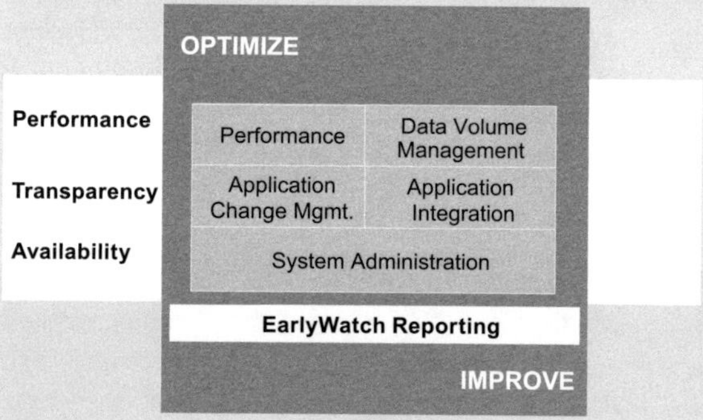

Figure 9 Service Groups in the Solution Management Optimization Class

- **Reduction of outlay for the administration of custom code**

  The SAP Modification Clearing service eliminates or encapsulates custom code.

- **Application Change Management**

  SAP Application Change Management services support you in the constant optimization of application change-management processes and the continuous implementation of changes.

- **Business Process Performance Optimization**

  This service analyzes your core business processes and gives technical and user-specific information on how they could be optimized. The service can also integrate special requirements for logistics or month-end closing.

  From a technical point of view, the optimization of the customer's own programs including SQL commands or Business Warehouse requirements is a particularly notable feature.

- **System Landscape Optimization (SLO)**

  The System Landscape Optimization Services are SAP's solution for the increasing demand for wide-scale changes in operational SAP NetWeaver solutions. These services make it easier to adapt your systems in line with business requirements and to align system landscapes effectively. There are many frequently occurring reasons for making changes to suit your business requirements, in ways that can be productized and automatically implemented to a high degree:

- Company mergers, acquisition, or sale of company business units
- Restructuring of the company organization
- Adjusting to proven business practices (best of industry) and /or IT strategies
- Reducing the complexity of IT landscapes

- **TCO Optimization**
  SAP has developed a TCO model with which you can create data about your own IT landscape. This is then analyzed and evaluated by SAP. SAP collates a report on the results of this analysis and evaluation that recommends procedures for reducing IT costs. SAP also uses the results data and analysis to improve existing procedures and to develop new ones.
- **Adaptive Implementation**
  As well as scoping the target landscape, these services also include the provision of a prototype development of an adaptive infrastructure and support for the switchover of complete system landscapes and the corresponding knowledge transfer.

Empowering

- **Optimization of your support organization**
  SAP Application Management Enabling and Empowering Assessment and other workshops help you to optimize the processes of your support and operations teams.

Tools

- **Change Request Manager**
  The Change Request Manager that is part of SAP Solution Manager is a tool for implementing the Change-Management process as part of an ongoing Problem-Management process. Changes can be managed, documented, reports made and, if required, transferred to the production system.
- **Performance optimization**
  The Self Services in the SAP Solution Manager identify potential for optimizing performance.
- **Virtualization of systems**
  The Adaptive Computing Controller is SAP's cross-hardware platform approach for the virtualization of your SAP systems and their centralized management.

3.2 IT Service Management

To support the business operations optimally, ITIL specifies that IT Application Management has to be tightly integrated with IT Service Management. IT Service Management usually comprises the processes in the Service Support and Service Delivery areas as well as operations added by SAP. Service Support designates all processes that can be viewed as operational. They encompass all tasks to be performed, such as processing malfunctions and changes or the integration of new configuration components. Service Delivery processes can be regarded as having a more strategic nature. They involve the planning, coordination and assuring of IT services, using suitable analyses and forecasts.

SAP has expanded this model with an operational area (see Figure 10). This covers several aspects that the ITIL model considers in other sections, such as IT Infrastructure Management or security. By contrast, ITIL is restricted to non-SAP-specific requirements. For example, the maintenance tasks and processes resulting from the general use of hardware and software are defined in ICT Infrastructure Management. SAP takes the view that there are some processes and tasks (in particular the use of SAP NetWeaver) that are fundamentally interwoven in IT Service Management, and direct integration is therefore a logical solution.

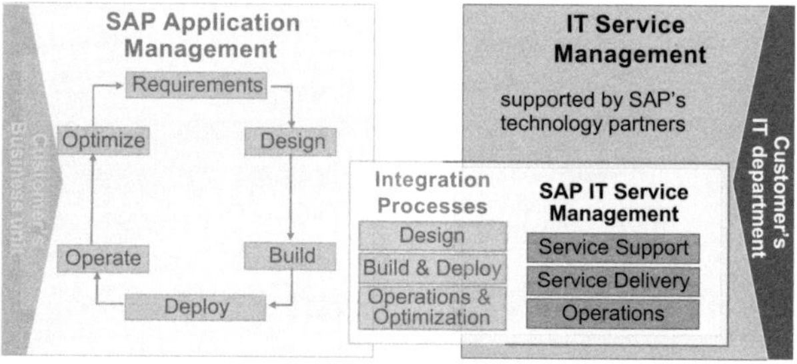

Figure 10 SAP IT Service Management in the Overall Structure

Figure 11 shows all of the processes of SAP IT Service Management. The following section will give a brief description of their content and purposes. Please read the pertinent ITIL literature for further information on the processes.

3.2.1 Service Support (in Line with ITIL)

The area of Service Support consists of five processes. Two of them form the function Service Desk. The Service Support area processes are inextricably linked with those of the Service Desk.

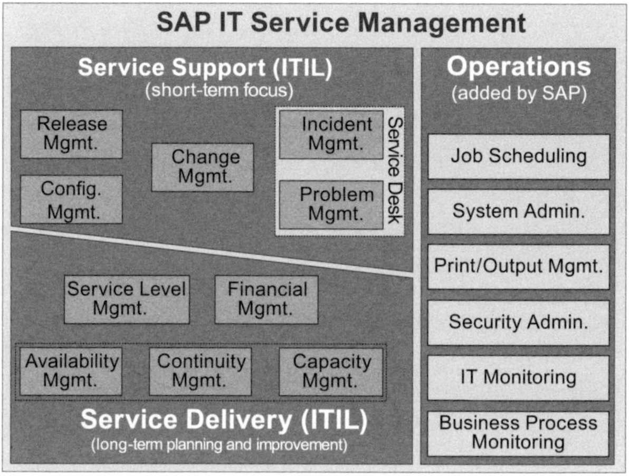

Figure 11 SAP IT Service Management in Detail

Service Desk Function

In addition to the Service Support processes, the Service Desk fulfills the function of the Single Point of Contact to IT Service Management. The idea behind this is that the end user should not have to use just any personal contact to obtain answers to his questions or problems. The Service Desk forms a central point of contact to record and check all incoming incidents. In this context, an incident is any interruption to Service Support, Delivery, and Operations that negatively affects business processes. One particularly important tool for handling incidents is the Incident-Management tool, also known as the Trouble Ticket Tool. From a strategic point of view, the Service Desk is also the best way of judging customer satisfaction. If it can be seen that an incident will result in the infringement of SLAs, the Service Desk will trigger defined escalation processes.

Incident Management

When the Service Desk receives notification of an incident and it has been classified pro forma, it is immediately forwarded to Incident Management. Here it is important to classify and prioritize incidents. The priority encompasses an estimation of the degree of urgency and the damage to the business process.

The main task of Incident Management is to restore normal operation as quickly as possible. From the point of view of Incident Management, this aim has been fulfilled when a way around the incident has been found. Incident Management does not analyze the cause of the incident. An important tool for Incident Management is a solution database where previous problems and their solutions or circumventions are documented. A suitable search engine is absolutely vital for this. If Incident Management cannot find a quick solution or circumvention of the incident, the incident is escalated to problem status.

Problem Management

The primary task of Problem Management is to discover the cause of the problem and to analyze it with a view to its solution. Its task then is to remedy the cause. This also involves judging how similar problems can be avoided. One way to do this is the careful documentation of the appearance, analysis, cause, and rectification.

Problem Management attempts to minimize the adverse effects of problems and breakdowns on business operations by proactively preventing errors, problems, and breakdowns, and by quickly and effectively resolving any problems that do occur. Problem Management includes documenting and classifying problems and errors, creating problem reports, and analyzing errors and trends. It may also be necessary to store solution strategies in the solution database.

The main difference between Problem Management and Incident Management is that Incident Management focuses on restoring service to users as soon as possible, whereas Problem Management focuses on preventing, fixing, and determining the causes of breakdowns. If it is not possible to remedy the cause, a request for change (RFC) must be opened. This means that the status is changed in the Trouble Ticket Tool, and responsibility switches to the Change Management process.

Configuration Management

The aim of Configuration Management is to identify, document, maintain, and verify all configuration items and their relationships to each other in a logical model of the IT infrastructure. The most important tool for this is the Configuration Management database, which contains the configuration items and their relationships. Items covered by Configuration Management include hardware, software and associated documentation, as well as the services to be provided for the user and the corresponding SLAs.

Change Management

In this context, a change means any modification to a configuration item or its relationship to other configuration items. Change Management is responsible for ensuring that the required changes for problem resolution, optimization, and continuous development are implemented using standardized methods and procedures and without adverse side effects. The RFC is then prioritized in terms of urgency and scope of damage and managed according to defined categories. There must be a balanced relationship between the need to make changes and any potentially damaging effects of those changes. All changes should be documented and tested. Their implementation should be planned, coordinated, and monitored carefully.

Release Management

Release Management controls the planning and monitoring of the successful implementation of new and changed releases as well as the corresponding hardware and documentation. One of the tasks of Release Management is the meticulous testing of new releases and training of users as well as the IT Service Management team, in particular those involved in the Incident Management and Problem Management processes. To determine the most suitable procedure for all technological components, you need a comprehensive overview of all dependencies.

Software release changes (upgrades) are always particularly critical if large quantities of essential business data are affected. This is usually the case in the SAP environment. It is important to remember that SAP systems frequently support the core business processes of companies. Therefore they are subject to special conditions with regard to availability. There is only very limited scope for planned system downtimes. This presents considerable difficulties for release upgrades. For this reason, this issue is a particular focus of support provided by SAP.

3.2.2 Service Delivery (in Line with ITIL)

The processes in the area of Service Delivery deal with planning and constantly ensuring the IT services.

Service Level Management

Service Level Management is responsible for defining, measuring, and reporting on appropriate KPIs, so that these KPIs can guarantee a stable, effective, controlled, and reliable operation of business processes. For this reason, key figures from business processes are frequently incorporated in technical requirements and key figures. Service Level Management defines the various areas and the scope of the SLA. This includes:

- Availability
- Performance
- Response and solution times in Incident, Problem and Change Management
- Escalation paths

Service Level Management is also responsible for adherence to existing SLAs, using monitoring and other appropriate tools. The analysis of the values measured in an important source of untapped optimization potential. Therefore correspondingly prepared reports (Service Level Reporting) must be provided for various target groups (management, users, persons responsible for IT).

Availability Management

The general aim of Availability Management is to ensure to the extent possible that services are available when the customer needs them. As such, Availability Management is concerned with optimizing the capabilities of the IT infrastructure. Availability is a term that covers a wide range of matters. The availability of an application is not necessarily synonymous with the technical availability of hardware or software. Availability Management must therefore provide a commonly accepted understanding of the availability of business processes. In this sense, availability consists of the following areas:

- Availability in the sense of time between downtimes
- Downtime prevention in the sense of resistance to incidents
- Serviceability, defined as the possibility of having support for the application performed by third parties. Put simply, persons other than the developer should be able to operate the new application.
- Maintainability in the sense of being able to implement changes during operation
- Security in terms of confidentiality, integrity, and usability

Availability Management's most important tasks are monitoring and creating reports on the key elements related to availability, creating forecasts and plans, and determining the availability requirements with regard to business interrelationships. An important tool for this is the Component Failure Impact Analysis (CFIA), that relates technical components and core business processes. The ways that downtime of a technical component effects the corresponding business process are analyzed, and solutions are considered for how this process can continue to be operated in emergencies using all available means.

Continuity Management

Continuity Management cooperates closely with Availability Management. Continuity Management involves the planning and implementation of disaster strategies (Service Continuity Plans). Continuity Management determines when the formulated disaster strategies must come into operation. The consequences of possible disasters or potential system downtimes are thereby kept to an absolute minimum in the defined environment.

The aim here is to be able to guarantee an agreed IT service level after a breakdown in business operations. Risk analysis and risk management can also be used to expose and reduce potential weak spots. You should not lose track of the costs and potential benefits during this. Increased investment in Availability Management and Continuity Management only make sense if the costs of downtime are greater.

Capacity Management

Capacity Management ensures that the available IT computational and storage capacities correspond to the current and future requirements of the company in terms of costs and speed. The ITIL Capacity Management also performs application sizing, whereby the application capacities are determined or estimated.

Capacity Management requires an understanding of the technical infrastructure and its capabilities, as well as the probable effects of introducing new assets and technologies.

Financial Management for IT Services

Financial Management for IT services delivers financial information for calculating the TCO and ROI. It can be used as a basis for decision-making and evaluating changes, such as IT investments. Since tasks and costs can be assigned, IT Financial Management can also be used for monitoring and managing the entire IT budget.

How SAP supports the Service Support and Delivery Processes

SAP supports you in the IT Service Management area with a wide range of services. This section describes only the most important services.

Services

- **SAP Solution Manager Starter Pack**
  This service is tailored to initial configuration and the first steps with the Solution Manager.
- **Adaptive Implementation**
  Adaptive Implementation services help you to distribute the resource requirements of applications over your existing computer capacities by virtualizing the SAP systems and by means of a central-management approach.

- **SAP Application Management**
  SAP Application Management services empower your support organization with expert help and problem solutions as well as in the continuous maintenance of the application and finding suitable KPIs in Service Level Management. This includes provisioning of support infrastructure and responsibility for the performance of the Service Desk function and the Incident Management, Problem Management, Change Management, Release Management and Service Level Management processes.
- **Upgrade Services**
  Figure 12 provides an overview of the most important services in the Upgrade environment. As every upgrade forms a project, it is possible to determine appropriate project phases. SAP offers services for the evaluation, planning, and implementation of upgrades. The services are tailored to customer requirements.
- **GoingLive for Functional Upgrade**
  As preparation for an upgrade, potential bottlenecks are located and optimization recommendations are given.
- **Safeguarding for Upgrade**
  This program supports you with the appropriate service in the development and implementation of the upgrade strategy.

Figure 12 ▶
SAP Service Portfolio for Upgrading to mySAP ERP

SAP Engagement	**PLANNING** Define transition/upgrade strategy and project plan
Complete Execution We deliver a complete solution	
Expert Guidance We solve key challenges	■ mySAP ERP Technology Workshop ■ SAP System Landscape Selection ■ SAP System Sizing ■ SAP Accelerated Value Assessment for mySAP ERP ■ SAP ValueAssessment ■ SAP Netweaver Reference Architecture Workshop ■ SAP ESA Roadmap Workshop
Quality Management We audit and provide directions	■ SAP Upgrade Assessment ■ SAP Quick Upgrade Evaluation
Enablement We provide knowledge & qualification	SAP Upgrade Empowering Ramp-Up Knowledge Transfer Solution Architect &
Product Maintenance We keep systems running and up-to-date	

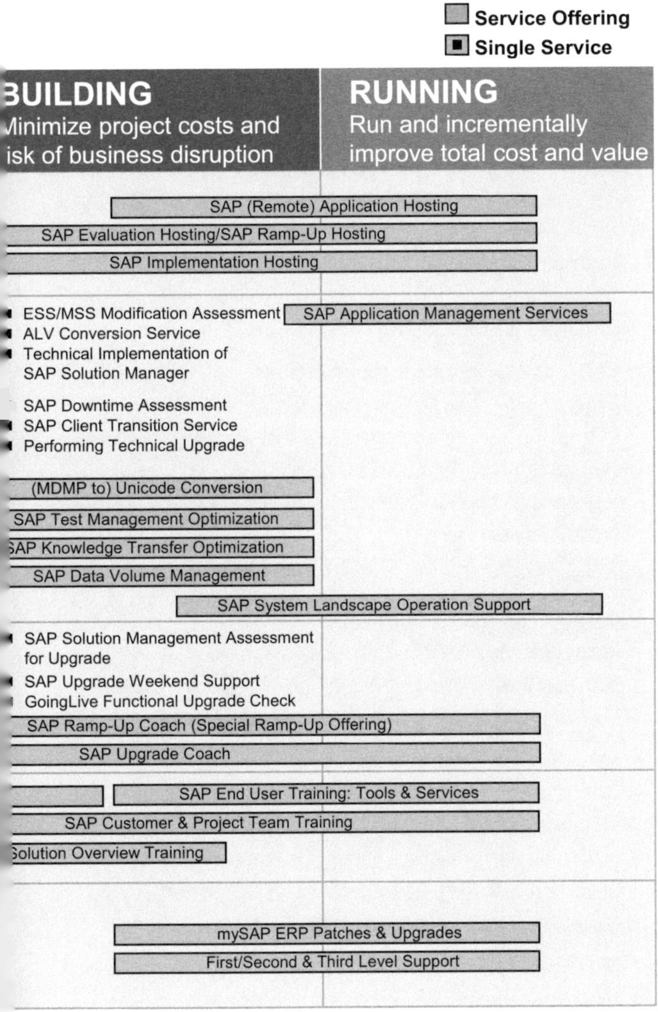
Service Offering
Single Service
BUILDING
Minimize project costs and
isk of business disruption
RUNNING
Run and incrementally
improve total cost and value
SAP (Remote) Application Hosting
SAP Evaluation Hosting/SAP Ramp-Up Hosting
SAP Implementation Hosting
ESS/MSS Modification Assessment
ALV Conversion Service
Technical Implementation of
SAP Solution Manager
SAP Downtime Assessment
SAP Client Transition Service
Performing Technical Upgrade
SAP Application Management Services
(MDMP to) Unicode Conversion
SAP Test Management Optimization
SAP Knowledge Transfer Optimization
SAP Data Volume Management
SAP System Landscape Operation Support
SAP Solution Management Assessment
for Upgrade
SAP Upgrade Weekend Support
GoingLive Functional Upgrade Check
SAP Ramp-Up Coach (Special Ramp-Up Offering)
SAP Upgrade Coach
SAP End User Training: Tools & Services
SAP Customer & Project Team Training
Solution Overview Training
mySAP ERP Patches & Upgrades
First/Second & Third Level Support

- **Release and Upgrade strategy**
  SAP Maintenance Assessment helps to define the correct release strategy and to make the optimum preparations for a planned upgrade.
- **SAP Software Change Management**
  Experts analyze your strategies in terms of software maintenance and development. The aim is to find the optimum design for the system landscape, Software Change Management process and release strategy. This can also involve training courses.
- **SAP Test Management Optimization**
  Every, change, every upgrade, and every new implementation requires an effective test strategy. This service aims to optimize test management. You require a reproducible, reliable test strategy that takes up as few resources as possible.

Empowering

- **Regional upgrade information in the SAP Service Marketplace**
  You can find country-specific information on upgrades on the SAP Service Marketplace.
- **SMO System Administration**
  This service supports you in particular during the implementation or switchover to new SAP solutions, providing an intensive training course focusing on new tasks and teaching Best Practices in the use of analysis monitoring and maintenance tools.

SAP supports you with a wide range of operational services. System services can be provided at your location or in one of SAP's data center to enable the fast use of the latest software functions (ramp-up) or for the upgrade or migration of existing solutions.

- **SAP Application Management Enabling**
  SAP Application Management Enabling supports the implementation of the Service Desk function as well as the Incident Management, Problem Management, Change Management, Release Management, and Service Level Management processes with expert knowledge and experience.

Tools

- **SAP Solution Manager**
  The SAP Solution Manager is the SAP tool for mapping the Service Desk function and the Incident, Problem and Change Management processes. In addition to managing the processes, the IT Service also has the task of solving problems. Many analysis, monitoring, and maintenance tools integrated in SAP NetWeaver support all IT service and support processes.

- **SAP Upgrade Roadmap**
  The SAP Upgrade Roadmap is the main guideline for the whole project team. SAP uses it to provide information on the current upgrade methods so that you can optimize the planning and implementation of your upgrade. Well-founded knowledge and a pool of experience are used to explain the functional and technical aspects of the upgrade of a complete system landscape.

- **SAP Adaptive Computing Controller**
  The Adaptive Computing Controller is the SAP solution for supporting the flexible and optimum utilization of existing resources.

3.2.3 Operations (Added by SAP)

Since IT operations ensure that your IT infrastructure runs in a highly reliable and predictable manner, SAP regards them as an essential part of IT Service Management. Operations concentrates on the regularly occurring tasks that must be executed manually or automatically. In particular, these are job planning, system administration, print and output management, and security administration. IT monitoring therefore has an important position in everyday work and can be seen as an independent area. All of these tasks are very much related to those of Application Management.

Job Scheduling

The term "job scheduling" designates the efficient processing of data at a predetermined time and in a prescribed sequence without user interaction. Job-scheduling strategies are important because of their impact on the system's resource utilization and response time affect core business processes.

Jobs of this kind do not run in a dialog, which is why they are frequently referred to as background jobs; therefore, there is a risk that these jobs are not monitored sufficiently. These jobs are frequently essential for business processes. Unlike the usual dialog steps within a business process, background jobs usually transfer much more data and are therefore more time-consuming. The challenge for the system administrator is to optimize the distribution of resources so that dialog processes, for example, are not adversely affected. There are frequently dependencies between the business process steps, meaning that background jobs are often subject to time and event conditions. SAP and other providers offer job schedulers separately for this purpose.

System Administration

Daily maintenance activities are an important part of ensuring the conditions of SLAs. System Administration therefore needs to define roles and schedule regular tasks (daily, weekly, monthly, and so on). It also has to establish procedures for non-scheduled tasks in the administration of users, systems, and databases. This also includes the regular checking of system logs and the analysis of unexpected problems found there. The aim of this is to automatically recognize as many incidents as possible and to respond to these if possible. To attain this objective, permanent analysis must be conducted and the tools required for this must be implemented.

Print and Output Management

A business process usually produces some kind of output, such as printed pages, electronic transactions, or e-mails. The extent to which the output process is essential to the business process depends on the business process itself. It is quite possible that the output can become a single point of failure for a business process. Outputs can also require particularly high security measures. Print and Output Management covers all the tasks required to deliver output in the right format at the right location and time with the appropriate security measures and the necessary availability. These include development and configuration activities to provide output, as well as operational activities that support the output flow with a sufficient degree of efficiency.

Security Administration

IT security ensures the confidentiality, availability, and integrity of data. This does not only concern the user administration of networks, operating systems, or databases. SAP systems provide special mechanisms to create and utilize complex authorization concepts for users. Security Administration must therefore ensure that unauthorized access to confidential data is not possible. On the other hand, it must also ensure that authorized users can call up the data at any time. This requires the authorization concept to be continuously adapted to organizational changes within the business processes. Additionally, the data needs to be accurate and may not be modified improperly.

IT Monitoring

From a system-management point of view, you should proactively create regular reports on the availability and performance of your systems and relevant areas, such as databases, memory consumption, and parameter settings. These requirements usually exceed the scope of Service Level Monitoring and Reporting. In this way you can uncover existing or potential bottlenecks caused by network limitations, server hardware, software components, resource-intensive database queries, or inefficient programming. Depending on the bottleneck, you should put together an action plan to optimize the system, as ultimately these bottlenecks can result in infringements of SLAs. A correlation of the accumulated quality criteria with the actual view of the system users is important in making business-relevant plans for sufficient support for the business processes.

Business Process Management

Business Process Management ensures that core business processes run smoothly and efficiently. This requires an understanding of business processes from the IT side, and an appreciation of system processes from the business side. Once critical processes have been identified, the next step is to look at the operations that affect them. These processes include scheduling, interface administration, and monitoring. Whereas SLM only defines, monitors and evaluates particularly important KPIs, the aim of Business Process Management is to monitor the entirety of business processes.

From a system and Business Process Management point of view, it is important to consider manageability, availability, performance, and integration.

- The tools and processes available to you should make the management of business processes and systems as simple as possible. They enable you to monitor your business processes and systems, to provide comprehensive support for users and to solve technical problems and difficulties in the system management area quickly.
- The technical infrastructure must have a sufficient capacity to meet the requirements for high availability. The tools and processes for monitoring the solution must ensure the fast detection of errors or delays in the process chain.

To react efficiently, you also need to be able to trace processes at document level.

- You require tools to measure and monitor the performance of the business processes on the basis of suitable KPIs defined in the SLAs.
- If your solution landscape consists of several software components connected by interfaces, you must ensure that the interface infrastructure runs optimally and smoothly. Therefore you should integrate the monitoring and the operation of these interfaces in your Application Management. To do so, you may also need tools and Best Practices to manage and integrate business processes across different applications.

How SAP Supports the Tasks in Operations

Services

- **Monitoring services**
  The creation of a monitoring infrastructure for the systems and applications is supported by various monitoring services during the planning, implementation, and subsequent operation of monitoring solutions on the basis of the SAP Solution Manager and by the integration of tools from third-party providers, if necessary.

Tools

- **Solution Life Cycle Management (SLCM)**
  SAP NetWeaver supports all phases of the software life cycles with optimized technology from the implementation stage to production operation, including later Change and Release Management. The tools and services of SLCM include:

- Installation, upgrade, and license management
- Tools and services for monitoring and problem analysis
- Test tools
- Customizing and configuration
- Data archiving

The Solution Manager is the central node for utilizing these tools.

- **Job scheduling**
  SAP provides Best Practices for complex and time-critical job scheduling. Together with SAP NetWeaver, SAP provides a job scheduler which takes Redwood Cranacle as a basis. The functionality far exceeds the transactions integrated to-date in mySAP solutions. In particular, cross-system job chains are supported.

3.3 Integration of SAP Application Management and IT Service Management

As well as processes and tasks that can be clearly assigned to IT Service Management and Application Management, there are also topics relating to the interface between the two areas. Application Management affects IT Service Management via these interfaces and vice versa. Therefore it is important to have a detailed view of the interfaces between the business and IT sides. The introduction of SAP NetWeaver based on an Enterprise Service Architecture (ESA) intensifies the requirements on these interfaces. SAP NetWeaver is the ultimate integration tool for processes, information and people, see Figure 13.

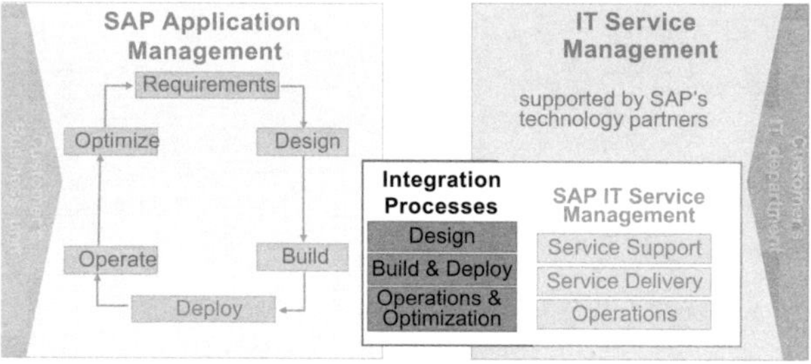

Figure 13 Integration in the Overall Structure

The following sections describe the most important interfaces between SAP Application Management and IT Service Management in the different life-cycle phases.

3.3.1 Integration in Design Phase

Design of the Technical Infrastructure

You must now draw up a suitable technical infrastructure based on the requirements of the solutions as compiled in the previous Requirements phase. You should plan the solution landscape and all its components in detail. As soon as you have compiled and derived all of the necessary determining conditions from the planned business-process design, you can complete sizing. It is recommended that you integrate the intended hardware supplier in this process, before you make a binding order for the necessary hardware.

The technical design of the infrastructure that supports your solution should comprise the following elements: servers, printers, network, front end, required configuration, and interfaces. In addition, you need to define strategies for the technical roll-out and for the required availability as well as determining the content of backup and recovery procedures, switchover/cutover, and disaster recovery.

Security Requirements

Security aspects must also be considered. This covers a variety of issues ranging from technical factors such as the network to authorization strategies within the systems. Output activities can also be subject to special security criteria, for example, HR payroll. These authorization and security requirements must be documented and planned into the technical implementation.

The estimations regarding the scope of business processes made in the Requirements phase are used to make an initial technical sizing for every component. You should make decisions at this early stage on the development system landscape including a client strategy.

Setting up the Project Infrastructure

You are now ready to set up the actual infrastructure and system landscape to support your project by performing the following steps: installation of the hardware and checking the technical environment, installation of the front end, installation, and configuration of the output devices for the project and the infrastructure for developing interfaces.

At this time, you also need to configure or build certain parts of your project infrastructure. These include configuration and testing of transport systems, the creation and configuration of the quality assurance environment, and the configuration and setup of the remote connection to SAP, as well as establishing system security and user security for the project team.

Supporting the Project System

Your project system and project environment are now ready for action. Regular administration of the systems is needed even at this early phase to ensure that the appropriate levels of performance and availability are guaranteed. The project systems need to be administrated and supported in a way similar to that of the production systems. The planned business processes are not yet active, but the systems can be regarded as in productive in terms of producing code, necessary customizing settings, etc. The business departments add their expectations for the production system in terms of availability, performance, and data security. This means that the administration must be planned for the following areas:

- Backup and recovery
- Transport landscape and concepts for change management
- Database administration
- Monitoring, including performance analysis
- Regular maintenance
- Security administration

- Output management
- Job scheduling

The procedure for technical support and the Service Desk includes the following:

- Installation of documentation and setup
- Integrating a Service Desk for the project
- Establishing communications and escalation procedures
- Definition of maintenance cycles and activities
- Defining the concept for operations and support

The key to running and supporting your solution successfully is to define operating procedures, roles, and skill profiles. On a general level, this involves reviewing the current support and monitoring strategies, as well as any SLA requirements and system-administration aspects. Once you have analyzed all of these areas, you can define all of the support requirements and formalize them. This will result in a set of clear procedures for support and, ultimately, a definition of the required process steps and elements of the support organization.

How SAP Supports this Phase
Services
▶ **Preparation for System Administration** The services in the SAP Solution Management Optimization program help you to implement efficient system administration procedures.

- **Service and Support strategy**
  SAP Application Management supports you in defining and validating the service and support strategy, creating the Support Service catalog, processes, structures and tools.

Empowering

- **Definition of operations and support strategy**
  SAP provides Best Practice documents for operations and support.
- **Solution Manager Starter Pack**
  Initial customizing and introduction to the Solution Manager.
- **SAP Security Guidelines**
  This is a collection of checklists for the most important security aspects with regard to the various SAP solutions. Additional information is provided for the implementation of security requirements.

Tools

- **Sizing**
  SAP Quick Sizer (Service Marketplace, alias *Quicksizer*) supports you in the definition and implementation of your sizings.
- **Reporting and documentation for project problems**
  SAP Solution Manager includes tools for reporting and documenting incidents and problems.

3.3.2 Integration in the Build and Deploy Phases

Building the Production Infrastructure

In the next phase, you implement the infrastructure for the production environment. A final site inspection of the data center facilities should include a review of the technical infrastructure, the procedures for communicating with the data center, and the operating procedures in the data center. The network infrastructure, including network monitoring, should already be established.

Now, the actual production environment can be set up. This involves installing back-end and middleware servers as well as the required software components. When setting up the database to be used in production at a later stage, pay particular attention to the configuration of the hard disks with regard to size and input and output activities, as these directly affect system performance.

Once you have built and configured the production environment, you need to install and configure output devices. The front-end software must be installed on the desktop systems. You can also implement the high-availability solution. Moreover, you have to implement your backup, recovery and disaster-recovery concepts at this stage. It is highly recommended to implement your security strategy at this point in time, covering both system and application security. This has the advantage that the implemented technology can be sufficiently tested and adjusted without problems before the start of production. After the production startup, configuration changes are much more difficult.

Authorizations and Security

You now need to implement the technology of the concepts for security administration developed in the previous phases. You need to remember that the initial security concept needs constant maintenance. New users will be added and user authorization profiles will have to be changed. You should implement suitable mechanisms and processes for this.

Test Planning and Execution

The planning and execution of tests involves more than just the functional aspects. To be able to judge an application as fully functional, you also need to test the operability, performance, and integration. The operator should plan appropriate tests and monitor their technical execution.

Cutover

The next task is to check whether the systems are ready for the cutover. A technical checklist will help to document the status of systems before and after the changeover to production operation. When conducting the system tests, make sure that you are working in a technically perfect system environment. A final load test, one that is as realistic as possible, will help you to judge if the configuration is suitable for the expected load.

Support

To ensure a smooth transition to the production environment, you must have support from implementation and technology experts in case any problems occur. This allows you to be certain that the cutover team can continue on schedule, while ensuring all problems are documented and resolved.

How SAP Supports this Phase

Services

- **Cutover services**
  SAP offers services which help your support organization during the transition from implementation to production. Tools, methods, and knowledge transfers are provided for user support. The focus here is on the required IT Service Management processes, their quality and the knowledge of staff members. The implemented processes are evaluated to check if they can sufficiently support the planned business processes. The results provide recommendations as to how potential bottlenecks can be reduced.
- **Interface Management**
  SAP Solution Management Optimization includes a service that verifies the technical stability of interfaces.
- **Performance**
  SAP Solution Management Optimization services improve performance by optimizing customer programs and the storage subsystem.
- **GoingLive Check**
  This remote service consists of three service sessions (analysis, optimization, verification). Two sessions are provided before production startup to analyze sizing and performance and to remedy potential bottlenecks in good time. The verification session makes an analy sis some time after production startup and refines the system configuration.

3.3.3 Integration During the Operations and Optimization Phases

Job Scheduling

IT-related issues concerned with job scheduling were discussed in the section on IT Service Management. In the context of integration, it is important to highlight the dependencies between the business requirements and IT. Today's operations often require 24/7 dialog processing. Background jobs and the work of dialog users must not be impaired by this. Performance must be at an acceptable level at all times. You need to define in detail what is regarded as acceptable. In addition, the results of such jobs have to be available promptly. A good understanding of business processes is vital for defining job nets—including the interdependencies between jobs—and ways to restart them in case of termination. IT Service Management needs to have a good overview and understanding of the business background.

Security Administration

IT-related aspects of security administration were also discussed in the section on IT Service Management. From an integration point of view, these aspects need to be aligned with user administration procedures in Application Management. Application security in the company is a key internal control component.

Elimination of Application Problems

Some application problems might have an impact on IT or vice versa. It follows, therefore, that application error processing needs to be tightly integrated in the Incident Management and Problem Management processes. Moreover, the IT departments and application support teams have to coordinate the procedures for resolving problems and implementing corrections. This calls for the integration of Service Desk processes and products.

Optimizing the System Landscape

Major changes to the underlying system landscape can become necessary during the solution's life cycle. Such changes are typically initiated to adapt to changing business strategies, such as centralization and divestitures, or simply to reduce the cost of an environment that has grown ever more complex. Changes to the system landscape normally necessitate data harmonization of business processes.

An often neglected potential for optimization can frequently be found in unnecessarily complex development and test system landscapes.

How SAP Supports this Phase

Services

- **Sizing validation**
  The SAP GoingLive Check enables you to check the planned solution landscape in terms of business volumes and configuration.

Tools

- **User administration**
  Central User Administration performs user administration tasks centrally and distributes the data to the systems in the solution.

- **Service Desk**
  SAP Solution Manager includes a Service Desk function that supports the application's users. If you use a different Service Desk tool, you can easily integrate it with SAP Solution Manager.

4 Summary

Figure 14 later in this chapter gives an overview of the key aspects of SAP IT Service & Application Management (ITSAM).

Compared with the ITIL approach, SAP IT Service & Application Management puts greater emphasis on the interaction of applications and operations. SAP regards IT service management as a service that is closely related to business processes. The special features and possibilities of SAP software required the introduction of the Operations area, where all services are listed that must be executed manually or automatically to maintain the typical ITIL IT Service Management and Application Management and that are closely related to these processes. In this way, Operations differs from the ICT Infrastructure Management, familiar to ITIL users, which focuses much more on the technical infrastructure.

SAP General Services
In addition to the services that are tailored to certain phases or processes in IT Service & Application Management, SAP also offers general services
Services
▶ **Hosting or Outsourcing** SAP supports you with a wide range of operational services. Demo systems or development systems can be

made available in the design and build phases and operated according to your requirements. Additional system services can be provided to enable the fast use of the latest software functions (ramp-up) or for the upgrade or migration of existing solutions.

The scope of outsourcing services in production operation ranges from infrastructure, including the administration and monitoring as part of Application Hosting, to the complete handling of application management for SAP solutions and their processes. This can include 24/7 support, high availability, and disaster-recovery scenarios for the optimum support of your business, even the remote operation of SAP systems in your own data center.

- **Implementation of Test and Integration Laboratories**
  The implementation of Centers of Competence (CoCs) for integration or quality assurance enables you to attain lasting increases in the quality of the solutions taken into production in complex landscapes with a high degree of integration. At the same time, CoC implementation will ensure the optimum level of utilization of the system resources made available for the project. The Integration Lab service supports you in the setup of such laboratories in your company. SAP can provide individual services or complete packages depending on your requirements.

Empowering

- **SAP Customer Competence Center (CCC)**
  SAP CCC is a special program to support the close cooperation between the support organization of SAP cus-

tomers and SAP itself. Certified CCCs have the option of participating in decision-making on matters relating to SAP product support and service development. SAP supports CCCs with detailed information and special programs for knowledge transfer. A generally higher level of qualification among CCC staff can be assumed, resulting in shorter solution times for the customer in the event of internal problem messages. This level of performance reduces the flow of messages to SAP. Messages from SAP CCCs are given priority by SAP.

- **Partner Competence Certification**
  Special certification programs are under development for the operation and support of SAP NetWeaver solutions. Staff with different profiles in the SAP IT Service & Application Management are trained. This practical knowledge can be proven with the certification.

You will have found by now that the SAP understanding of quality and quantity in IT Service Management in the phases of Application Management is very much in line with the common understanding of ITIL. Enhancements and details have been added to cater to the special characteristics of SAP solutions. SAP offers a wide range of services, training courses, and tools for the various tasks involved over the life cycle of a solution and for process implementation and execution. Only the most important of these have been presented in this pocket guide. Other offers are available from the SAP Service Marketplace, or you can contact SAP for more details.

Figure 14 ▶
Interaction Between SAP Application Management and IT Service Management

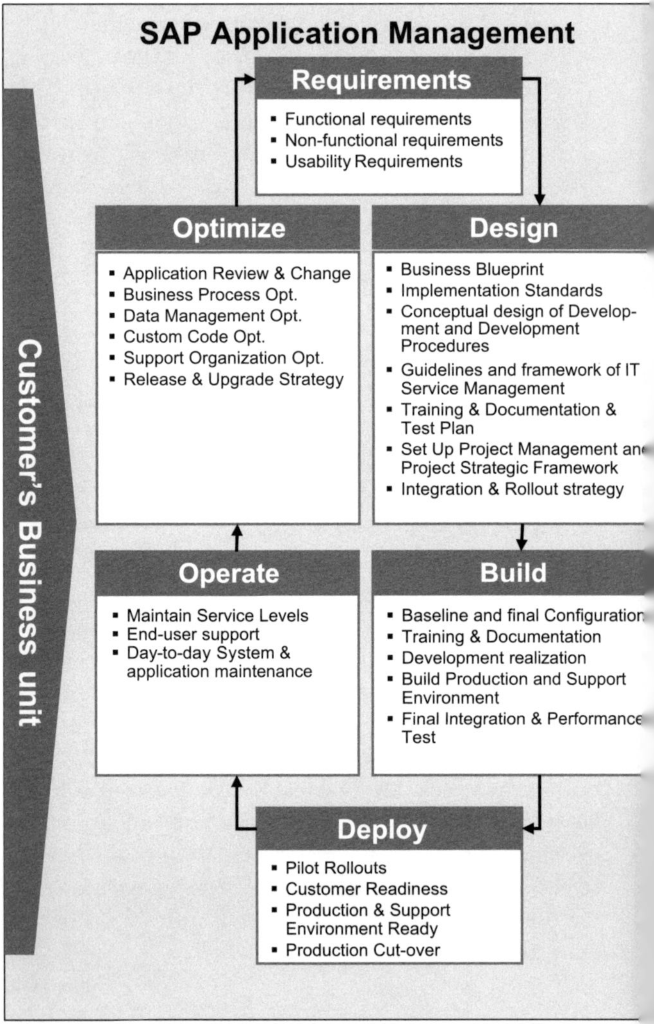
SAP Application Management
Customer's Business unit
Requirements
Functional requirements
Non-functional requirements
Usability Requirements
Optimize
Application Review & Change
Business Process Opt.
Data Management Opt.
Custom Code Opt.
Support Organization Opt.
Release & Upgrade Strategy
Design
Business Blueprint
Implementation Standards
Conceptual design of Development and Development Procedures
Guidelines and framework of IT Service Management
Training & Documentation & Test Plan
Set Up Project Management an
Project Strategic Framework
Integration & Rollout strategy
Operate
Maintain Service Levels
End-user support
Day-to-day System & application maintenance
Build
Baseline and final Configuratio
Training & Documentation
Development realization
Build Production and Support Environment
Final Integration & Performanc
Test
Deploy
Pilot Rollouts
Customer Readiness
Production & Support Environment Ready
Production Cut-over

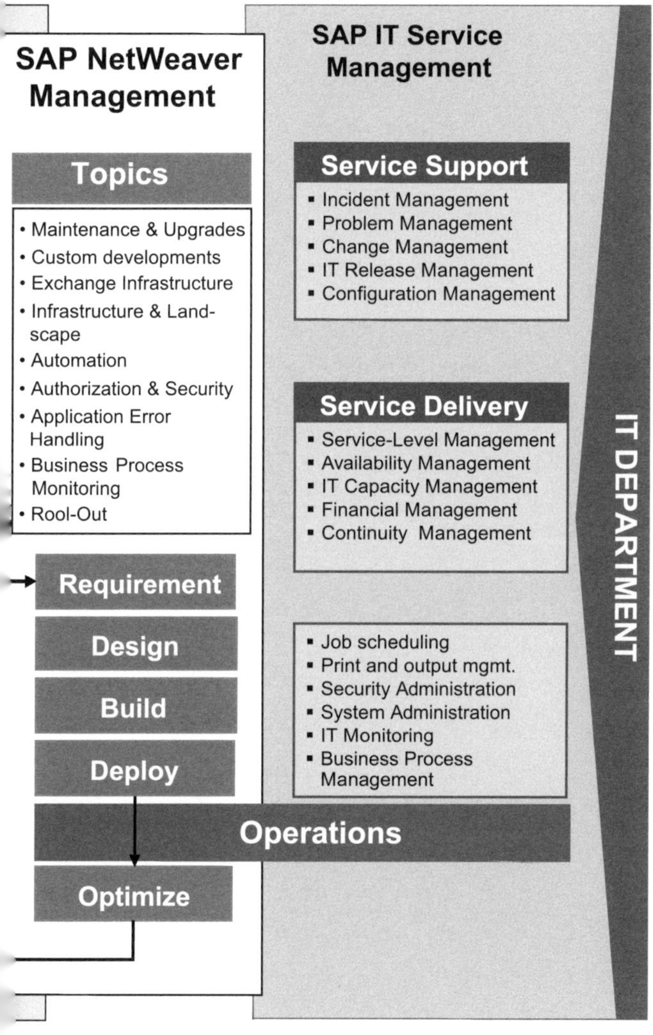
SAP NetWeaver Management
Topics
• Maintenance & Upgrades
• Custom developments
• Exchange Infrastructure
• Infrastructure & Land-scape
• Automation
• Authorization & Security
• Application Error Handling
• Business Process Monitoring
• Rool-Out
Requirement
Design
Build
Deploy
Operations
Optimize
SAP IT Service Management
Service Support
▪ Incident Management
▪ Problem Management
▪ Change Management
▪ IT Release Management
▪ Configuration Management
Service Delivery
▪ Service-Level Management
▪ Availability Management
▪ IT Capacity Management
▪ Financial Management
▪ Continuity Management
▪ Job scheduling
▪ Print and output mgmt.
▪ Security Administration
▪ System Administration
▪ IT Monitoring
▪ Business Process Management
IT DEPARTMENT

Index